# *L*EAVING
## HOLDS ME HERE

# LEAVING HOLDS ME HERE

## SELECTED POEMS 1975 – 2000

## GLEN SORESTAD

### SELECTED AND EDITED BY JOHN NEWLOVE

THISTLEDOWN PRESS

Canadian Cataloguing in Publication Data

Sorestad, Glen A., 1937 –
Leaving holds me here

Poems.
ISBN 1-894345-32-0
I. Title.

PS8587.O746A6 2001   C811'.54   C2001-910250-X
PR9199.3.S575A6 2001

Cover painting, *Improbable Possibilities #2* by David Alexander

Typeset by Thistledown Press Ltd.
Printed and bound in Canada

Thistledown Press Ltd.
633 Main Street
Saskatoon, Saskatchewan  S7H 0J8
www.thistledown.sk.ca

## ACKNOWLEDGEMENTS

Thistledown Press thanks Ekstasis Editions for permission to reprint poems from *Icons of Flesh* and *Today I Belong to Agnes,* and Harbour Publishing for poems from *Jan Lake Poems* and *Air Canada Owls.* We also thank Hawk Press (*Stalking Place*) and Writers of the Plains (*Birchbark Meditations*).

The author acknowledges and appreciates John Newlove's expert editorial direction in the selection and presentation of the poems for this volume.

Thistledown Press gratefully acknowledges the financial assistance of the Canada Council for the Arts, the Saskatchewan Arts Board, and the Government of Canada through the Book Publishing Industry Development Program for its publishing program.

# CONTENTS

## POEM FOR SONIA

I would never write another poem
if only I could show you
in a few perfect lines
what the touch of your fingers
on my aging cheek
means

*from* WIND SONGS

RED FOX IN FALL

This red fox
         we have set to flight
is a flash fire
         against
the dying gold
         of the wheat stubble:
a short moment
         and we are not certain
there ever was
         a burning motion
in the fading fall
         light
that closes now
         around us.

## DRY SUMMER

The August heat leans from the sun
The wind whispers dry apologies
The wheat droops its heavy heads

looks to the cracked earth for water
The sun burns each head with its glare
The sun singes the wind's breath

The dusty wind croaks, maybe tomorrow
The wheat answers, we hope so
The sun glares in silence

The sun drops in the wooded hills
The wind slides away to the east
The whispers echo, maybe tomorrow

Night comes softly with cool fingers
Night says nothing to the earth
Night is a nurse on soft soles

The wind returns before dawn
does a dance through the wheat
The wind says, I told you so

The wheat turns its heads to the east
The whispering spreads the word around
The scent of rain washes the wind's face

80 03

*from* PRAIRIE PUB POEMS

THE WINDSOR HOTEL, BUCHANAN

Two farmers sit at separate tables
            in silence
their backs to one another
the only patrons of the moment.

The question of an irrigation ditch
            divides them
and has for ten silent years
of back-to-back neglect.

Their harvest — grain and children
            grown and gone
wheat and barley, sons and daughters
grown and gone, east and west.

Soon they will have only
each other and the silence.

BEER AT COCHIN

The lazy August fire
                    wanted quenching.
    Even the slightest breeze
                    from the lake
could not suppress the knowledge
that Cochin pub was near
and cool
        and wet.

Entering the dim-cool
                    (alive
with beer promises) room is
so good
        you want to stop
                            forever
the moment
            to hang suspended.

    The Indians and Métis have their own
    section in the pub at Cochin —
    no cordons
                no signs
                            no markers
        of any kind
        no, nothing so blatant.
        But in Cochin
        they know
                    where to sit.
Everyone in the room knows
                            even you
    total stranger
                    even you know too.

But you ignore it and sit down
next to a table of Indians
                              and wait
and it doesn't take long
                    no
not long at all.

Someone flips a switch
                    and conversation
in the room is silenced —
and even the table next to you
is frozen.

And the bartender comes over
                              his face pained
and he asks
            if you wouldn't like to
            move closer to the bar

and you are well aware
that it isn't really a question
                    now
or ever.

## THE HOTEL IN ITUNA

Outside the wheatfields roll like a Commons speech
rocking green-gold in the shortening of summer
and the wind sucks the tongue as dry as noon.

Inside the hotel a mural stretches the long wall
into a Hawaiian beach, hand-painted by an Indian
who saw the picture once on an American postcard.

# FORT HOTEL, FORT QU'APPELLE

Smoke slides up the building and out
through dust-streaked windows into the night.
In minutes its fiery spasms break
the back of winter's frigid grasp,
back parka-bundled watchers away
like a spurt of August oozing down
from the surrounding hills.

       Evenings in July we sat around the table —
       A curious motley company of instructors
       in art, writing, music, pottery, dancing
       drawn to the Valley's sticky closeness,
       bound together in a strange alliance
       by a table full of frothy lager —
       a piper from Scotland, a concert tenor
       from Toronto, a clarinetist from Utah,
       an actor from somewhere, leaning together
       as night pushed the Qu'Appelle hills
       down and over our table of beer.

They may rebuild the old Fort as it was
brick by brick, restore its likeness. Perhaps.
But see these blackened ruins,
charred memories burned in the fires of time.
Even words on pages become trite.

## VAL MARIE HOTEL

Val Marie under the noon sun
sweats and a tired black dog
pants on the front porch
of the hotel.
        We walk up and down
the town's disappearing business block
shooting photos of another prairie town's
decay.
        One of the remaining merchants,
third generation of shopkeepers here,
spots us, beckons us into his store,
provides us an oral local history
including the only photo extant
of the original Val Marie Hotel
shuddering in flames and smoke.

        When we enter the Hotel it is just past noon
        but the pub's three patrons show
        marks of a prolonged bout.
        One is a merchant who is arguing
        with a customer who wants him
        to open his place for business.
        The other two are farmers who
        have stayed overnight in town
        and are now stretching out each drink
        as if it might be the final one.

The merchant's wife settles one issue
with her stormy arrival
and her husband's hasty departure.
One of the farmers comes over,
joins us at our table; his partner

converses with the empty chair
across from him for fifteen minutes,
gets agitated with his own remarks
or the silence from across the table
and leaves. But old Lucien,
now at our table has no reason to go
so he regales us with Dirty-Thirty yarns
about trapping skunks for beer money.

"You want to see de rattle?"
old Lucien asks, when we inquire
about prairie rattlers around here.
"I got de rattle den on my farm.
"I show you de rattle —
lots of dem!" We decline,
polite but firm, having no desire
to follow a wobbly Lucien
through any rattlesnake dens.

"One time I was drive de fencepost
wit de sledgehammer, you know
and de rattle, he come up behind me.
I tink he want to find out
what de hell I'm doing dere.
When he rattle his tail behind me,
by god, de hat she jump
right off my head!"

Finally we leave old Lucien alone
and the Val Marie Hotel grows silent.
Outside the sun is burning the world
and the old black Lab still lies,
tongue lolling, on the front porch.

# HOTEL AT HAFFORD

A large scale model
of an Air Canada Lougheed Tri-Star
suspended by thin wires
hovers above the bar
like a helicopter.
The almost imperceptible
movements of the jet liner
are still a distraction
more compelling than
any woman's breasts:
this red and white
toy the object
of the youthful
bartender's daydreams,
his eyes drawn
to the model aircraft
at every lull in his work.

He reaches into the cooler,
draws three cold pilsener,
explodes the caps with deft
flicks of his wrists
against the wall opener
like a pilot snapping
control levers and switches
in preparation for take-off.

As he rings up three beer
his eyes stray upwards and I
can almost hear the voice
inside his head saying
*Fasten your seatbelts, please.*

ဆ ၛ

*from* PEAR SEEDS IN MY MOUTH


THE BADGER

Something in the early morning sun
that strides across the stubble
newly uncovered from winter snow
takes me somewhere
south of Wood Mountain
driving a gravel backroad
in fast waning light,
seeking the wily cock pheasant —
the day's perfect end.

>    But instead, the last light
>    captures badger, ambling unconcerned
>    about his shrinking world,
>    sunbeams splashing his silver coat
>    making him a miniature grizzly bear
>    in a world of stubble and sky.

Now, this morning, somewhere north
as sun turns last year's stubble
to the near-gold of autumn
I recall the badger,

animal of rare boyhood days,
and I wonder whether sometime
there will be another badger
somewhere to reawaken lost memories
here
in this country of growing myths.

# JUST A KID IN VANCOUVER

Just a kid in Vancouver
  pulling a wagonload of dreams
    down East Broadway,
  tossing spiny-coated chestnuts
    at passing streetcars,
  retrieving pancaked pennies
    after the streetcar passed.

The kid wheeled his wagon
  down gravelled alleys screaming
    off to his latest four-alarm fire,
  scaring the Japanese fish-peddlers
    plying their back-alley salmon,
or sometimes he clanked down sidewalks
  a victorious tank rumbling from the war
    just over but not forgotten,
occasionally a four-wheeled fruit truck
  leaving the neighbour's apple tree,
    one-legging away his booty.

The kid in Vancouver is gone now,
as is the tousled farm boy he became.
Only in the sporadic dreams of a sleeper
is there still a kid in Vancouver
  pulling a wagonload of dreams
    down East Broadway.

PUBERTY RITE

First date:
sitting in the backseat of a '49 Chev
with a big-breasted Polish girl
two years older
a hundred years more experienced
saying things
that she would somehow manage to finish
trying to recall
what all those paperback lovers said
failing to remember.

After the movie:
driving back home
night now a blessing
to conceal the awkwardness
the indecision, the hopeless inadequacy
babbling about the movie
until she has to stop your lips
with hers
guide your clumsy sweaty hands
with hers
and you tremble
with a perfect joy
that can never
be equalled.

The next day:
you believe your voice is deeper
more manly, more mature
and you wonder if anyone around
will notice the difference.

# HAWK ON A TELEPHONE POLE

I drive by your perch slowly on the tractor.
Your eyes rotate to follow me in passing,
unblinking, without a hint of fear,
the quiet indifference of the hunter.
You are sated for the moment, at rest,
Except for the unflinching eyes
you could be merely an extension
of the lifeless telephone pole.

It is not easy to see you now,
roosted like some barnyard fowl,
the clawed killer of the sky,
dropping out of the sun
to ravage a field mouse
with terrible talons.

Except for the pent-up fury
of those slowly moving eyes
that follow me down the road —
and a long time after.

## McGILLIVRAY'S PEAR TREE

A pear tree grew in Tom McGillivray's yard,
a tree from which we kids were not allowed
to pick — not one experimental bite.
We could pick apples, cherries, any fruit,
but not the fruit from this enchanted tree:
for so it was for us, unknowing of
society's strange dictates and demands.

Then one dark night while old McGillivray slept,
unlearned in the letters of the night,
I slipped into his yard. Beneath that tree,
uncertain of what perils might befall,
I tasted the forbidden pear; the taste
confirmed my going out that quiet night.
Since then I've lived with pear seeds in my mouth.

## SITTING ON A HIGH BANK
## OVER THE SOUTH SASKATCHEWAN RIVER

It seems I must content myself to be
a poet of quiet places and gentle hands
of sun-streaked sky and rough-edged voices
dusty prairie towns and wind-burned faces
everything so commonplace and familiar

because

in wild hair I'd be a derelict
the voice of outrage doesn't suit me
I don't want to be a writer-in-residence
I'd rather read someone else's poetry aloud
no relatives of mine were tortured by the SS
my hackles do not rise at the word *Communism*
I haven't been ripped off by my family doctor
and my wife seems determined to be constant.

Of course

I could write about the ugliness I hear
from the scattering of cynics I know who
sleep with the radio on all night for fear
of missing out on the latest juicy atrocity
or I could make up a list of miseries
so that I could join the legion of bitchers
who have nothing to offer but a rotten core
having already eaten the apple themselves.

Therefore

leave me to my stubbled ignorance because
I see more laughing eyes more reason to celebrate
than to sing dirges for mankind or to kick
the legs out from under a dancing man.

*from* ANCESTRAL DANCES

ANCESTRAL DANCE

The violin my grandfather
staunchly called a fiddle
but refused to play for us
held for him some magic link
with the man he was.

Left at home alone when we
were safely distant for the day
he'd uncase the fiddle,
rosin the bow with trembling fingers.

Caught in the mystery of the past
he delayed death, bowed the fragments
of a life that was always private,
even on a crowded dance floor.

In the gathering silence
of seventy years
with fumbling recall he
became the dance.

## REFLECTION

Today my grandfather's bones ache.
My father's back is stiff.
And the ghosts of both
look back at me
while I shave.

LEAVING
*(for Ernest Dalshaug 1922-42)*

You board the evening train in Buchanan,
not yet twenty.
You can not know these rails
are a bayonet blade
into the bowels of Normandy.

You look back into the faces,
the mirror of all you know
before you swing aboard,
ride your uncertainty
into a distant dawn.

That last backward glance
into the eyes and faces
that will you a safe return
makes you recoil,
explode with a vision:

      a soldier, crumpled on a stony beach
      wears your face, lips twisted
      in a final cry, your last breath
      wheat chaff whirled on the wind.

"I won't be back, you know.
I'll never see you again," you cry
as the train slowly drags you away.

SHITEPOKE

shikepoke / sloughpump
shike/poke   slough/pump
shitepoke   shitpoke
what does it matter now?

    shikepoke or sloughpump
    the memory fades  fades
    we name and then unname
    but it was our word   good enough
    for anyone but ornithologists
    who latinize the bird world

the plains Cree named it
*moo-ku-hoo-sew*
naming the evening sound
when an Indian says the name
you can smell summer slough

and the first French trader
named it *butor*   then plunged
his paddle deep to pass by

    does it really matter
    that this bird
    is really the *yellow bittern*
    (though no one I know
    ever heard or used this name)?

we didn't know that shitepoke
was some English settler's way
of naming the bird
that shits when it leaps
to flight from the slough

I can still hear
the pump-handle sound cut the evening
still mould in my throat
the shitepoke sound

shikepoke / sloughpump
you are my language my image
shike/poke  slough/pump

FACES

I only know you
as you are now

not the young woman
who turned men's heads
made their blood leap
like a vaulting deer

You smashed
through the car's windshield
your face
a sudden frightened explosion
of glass shards

They wheeled you to the surgeons
masked in bandages
built you a new face
made you another woman
for another lover

a woman
who dreams each night
in that other face

# ELEGY FOR SONDRA

Saturday night you were one of us;
today a sudden fear makes us turn
our faces aside in school corridors,
throats too tight to trust with words.

The awful silence of your dying alone,
school chants that echoed within you
only hours before on the basketball court,
is a grim irony we bear — mute.

Today at the funeral the other cheerleaders
stand silent, gaudy pompoms laid aside;
the basketballers, lank, white-shirted,
shift nervously in this unfamiliar rite.

The silence of earth is now your silence,
after which there is neither dirge nor cheer.
There are other games, other silences,
but none so still as that which lingers here.

FOR NELSON SMALL LEGS, JR.

After the last creative act, then what, Coco?
Wherever you are do you dream
winds of protest ripping through federal corridors,
bureaucrats aquiver like prairie grasses
in the first wind? Do you dream
your people rising united from ashes
of long-dead campfires,
ancestral strength renewed?

In that shadow world, Coco,
are all visions shaman-sharpened?
I see your lonely gesture before me:
the desperation of the final moment,
the protest after which there can be
no other . . .

Your father's Peigan death chant
has become wind again at Pincher Creek,
the wailing of the women stilled.
In the silence of this alien Catholic churchyard,
away from the hill you chose
for your final sleep, your brothers
of every song taste the bitterness
of your dance of death.

# CREE FISHING GUIDE

I light my cigarette
notice your eyes
fixed on the pack
offer you one
which you take

I light a match
we share
then return
to our roles:
you, the guide
me, the fisherman

I think of treaties
neither of us
ever signed

# JAN LAKE

George, our silent Cree guide
cuts the outboard motor
as we troll slowly past a rocky point
wordlessly allows the boat
to drift towards the shoreline
I think:
*George is hungry, so it's lunchtime*
*George thinks it's time to stretch our legs*
*George needs to take a piss*

We drift towards a clump of willow
jutting like an afterthought from the rock
and George seems intent on something
I look eagerly but see nothing at all
The boat touches the rocks of the point
and at last we see the three large eggs
camouflaged in their feathery nest
We stare in silence

*Loon*, George says softly
and starts the motor again

The old Woodland Cree in the filleting shed
watches our slow butchery of fish
and finally says to us
*Here, I show you howta fillet*
*d'walleye, dere's nuttin to it atall.*

He grasps a plump walleye by the head
pulls his filleting knife from its sheath
makes several quick passes behind the gills
slashes the belly open, slices the side
strips back one side of fish from head to tail
in a flash of fillet, flips the fish over
and flakes the other fillet.
Knives and fish hold no secrets for him.

But we, mouths agape like pike-strikes
disbelievers at an illusionist's show
stare, try to peel away some small deceit
something that will explain it all.

*See dese bones here? Watch.*

He flips the fillet meat-side down
places his thumb on the scales above the bones
slides his knife under the fillet
along the filleting table under the pressure
of his thumb with a soft snick
lifts the fillet, shows us the bones
a neat sliver lying on the table.

*Y'see. Nuttin to it. Now you do it.*

He grins again and walks away
wiping his knife blade on his jeans.

LISTENING

Rain voices mutter
    on garden leaves
in the darkness

Down the alley
    a cat's sudden squall

In the distance
    a police siren

I return to the house
    out of the darkness
to face my unkindness
    in the light's glare

# FROST WARNING

Last night we argued
over whether to cover the garden —
protect the delicate tomatoes,
the fragile cucumber vines,
whether the bruising of tender plants
caused by discarded sheets and clothes
was worth the effort, knowing
early frost was a slim risk.

But you are a practical woman,
not given to gambles,
and I am the poker player.

We compromised as usual:
you went out and covered the plants

It didn't freeze and this morning
we are both happy, both winners.
I guess that's how it's always been.

# THE LAST KNOWN PHOTOGRAPH OF MARY BEAR

In winter night headlights confined
to an illusory patch of reality,
the driver is lulled by heater warmth,
brunts the drowsy darkness.
On the straight gravel road a glare
of sealed beams stabs the night.

The darkness is torn apart —
a figure on the road's edge totters,
hand raised to meet the crushing thud,
the figure hurled aside
down the embankment
to its final pose.

The car, stopped, throbs in the cold.
The camera has already rejected the last known photo
of Mary Bear, age twenty-eight,
one arm outstretched, mouth agape
eyes locked in a silent scream.

FATHER

You lay awake
and twisted with your doubts
called yourself a failure
because you never could
become what all your friends
believed you should

Deep within the guts
you thought you lacked
the murderous cancer host
charged every tear

And after you were still
the last song lost into dark
then and only then
could my eyes see

POEM IN A RESTAURANT

If I could have written a poem
on the back of a dollar-laden conversation
I would have

(when you walked in
the silver on my tongue
turned to lead
your eyes burned
across the years between us
with the pale fire
of silent questions)

I failed then
but I move now
across the after-silence
kiss your darkened eyelids
with words

80 03

*from* JAN LAKE POEMS

SPRING SNOW

Morning breaks cold, slumps
like a slicker on the black spruce.
Grey sky mutes the early light.

We rise from warm beds to fish
and through the cabin windows
watch the first drift and sift of flakes.

Against the dark spruce white
flakes, cotton patches parachute
soundless to the needled earth.

This unwanted intrusion of winter
numbs, draws us from the window
to enclose each other in our warmth.

Then the snow ceases, silent
as its beginnings. The ground betrays nothing.
We open the door to spring and fish.

MATINS

The lake lies before us, winter's reverie
where distant shorelines are fringes of waking.

Our boat skims over unseen life below
to pools where dreams and fish run deep.

I trail my hand in the passing water's cold,
feel the numbness like cold day breaking.

Dreams are fish that swim through our nights,
cold ghosts that swirl throughout our winter sleep.

RITUALS

The assembly of rod and reel:

bolt the reel into place,
run line through the eyes
of the rod, knot the leader
to unyielding snugness,
then the walleye jig, a lead head.
The frozen minnow impaled
on the single barbed hook.

The first deliberate cast.

The slow sinking of the line,
quelling the impatience, the desire
to rush the lure back to the boat,
the silent counting before the retrieve.
The jerky retrieval of the lure,
picturing the minnow on the bottom
darting forward in quicksilver flashes.

Waiting for the moment, waiting
for the sudden lurch of the rod,
the arcing fibreglass,
the tremor that vibrates
from fingers to shoulders.

Waiting for the first fish.
Waiting for the memory,
the reawakening.

## REEFS

Below placid surfaces lie
fists of rock. Unseen

they wait like anger, quick
to destroy the rash.

Indian guides have learned
avoidance of these reefs. We

name this history. We try
to fathom their internal maps,

but like our words, our vision
fails us.

## THE HUSTLERS

Forrie and I have held the pool table
at the Jan Lake bar for too long now
it's plain to see.
There are mutters, hard glances
begrudged dollar bills
stacked on our table, an untidy pile
while we reel in our fortune
like sailors on shore leave.

But Ernie has already lost twice to us
and now prompted by two whites
slams the cue ball into a pocket
(a move that is far from friendly)
knowing that his opponent must hit
the black ball shooting up and down
using one of the sloppy cushions
or lose the game.

I must face this ploy
and I know it's no joke
not just a shot to leave me tough.
It's a warning to Forrie and me
that we've been here long enough
and we'd be wise to pack it in.

Every eye in the place is on me
to see how well we've paid attention
and the sudden silence is deafening
as I step to the table to shoot.

So I listen carefully — and miss the shot.

There's a happy explosion of table-talk.
We pay off Ernie and his partner
and Ernie averts our eyes:
he's had more satisfying victories.

But we've listened so well
(and like the sight of our own blood so little)
that we take our stack of ones and buy beer
send it around to the tables of losers
and a much more healthy hum
fills the smoky air when we sit down
and we know we won't have to listen
for footsteps behind us when we leave.

# NUMBER ONE GUIDE

## 1.

Fifty-six years he has beaten
a life from these dark woods
with a Harper's Island trapline.
And fifty-six summers here
on Jan as boy and man,
            fisherman and guide.

"I'm number one guide,"
                    John shouts.
And who can question this?
He has forgotten more about this lake
than any *moonie-ass* can dream
or ever hope to learn.

But years of booze have bent John
like a rough wind. Lodge owners
hire him now only
                as a last resort.

## 2.

Forest fires have swept
the camp of all Indian guides, all
but John, here, with the women
and children. His age and condition
a comfortable reprieve
from days and nights of smoke
and heat, and endless shovels.

So John is Jan's sole guide:
transformed from last year's pariah
to this year's saviour, besieged
with requests and promises.
American twenties and bottles
of Old Crow swirl around him
like the dangerous drift of smoke.


3.

In the morning the camp rises
on Seewup time and John heads
his flotilla of American boats
strung behind like empty promises
to Deschambault River.
                              We decline
his offer to follow him,
                              prefer
to map-read our own route
alone to Grassy Narrows where
we will find other walleyes.
John throws us a jaunty wave
and captains his armada away.


4.

Early afternoon. We have returned
with our limits of walleyes.
John returns with seven boats,
all babbling about *grayet nathren piehk*.

John has been liberally plied with booze.
He has little desire to fillet fish,
looks instead for a beer or whiskey.

He tells us of last winter. Falling
through the ice. His narrow escape.
How his son caught him by the hair,
somehow managed to pull him out.
"By the hair!" he roars, running
his hand through his dark hair.
"John was *THAT* close!" he shouts.


5.

We show John our map. Where
we have fished. The spot at the Narrows.
Mark it as closely as possible,
indicate where we caught our limits.
John grins. Nods his approval.
But our black X seems to stir something.
He grabs the pen.
                    "Look. I show you!
Best walleye spot.
P.P. Walleye. Look here.
This one right here . . . "

He X's a point on our map.
" . . . my favourite. P.P. Walleye."
The X is just off Harper's Island.
His winter grounds.
                    "Here's another.
And this one too."

There are now four X's.

His excitement dies. He stares,
seems embarrassed at his marks.
Finally, "Don't tell nobody."
A sadness has taken over.
"You go there. But don't tell
nobody I showed you."
                              Subdued,
he wanders away to his camp,
away from something he understands
and would rather forget. Somehow.

VESPERS

Against the fade of light
the spruce line
the lake with dark.

Spectral birch slink
into boreal night
and spruce reach
their ragged arms
to bring down the light.

৪০ ০৪

# *from* Hold the Rain in Your Hands

ONE MAN

The easy laughter is gone now.
Face pinched, a darkness has settled
for John. Last year his son. Dead,
victim of another's jealousy, cut
down by a shotgun blast at a party.
A few days ago, his sister,
one who was closest, gone.
John wears his grief in his eyes
as long as he can. Then breaks
as we all must. As we must
wear his grief with us
this night, and tomorrow,
carry it away when we leave.
There is no other way.

## THE RETURN

The song of return
is not the song of journeys out.

We are tired, our faces burn
with unaccustomed wind and sun.

Fish fade from our minds.
The talk is low, desultory.

Long silences settle and bind,
a closeness comfortable as praise.

In hours we will be back within the maze,
our other lives.  Another spring, and north.

## SASKATCHEWAN TOWN AT NIGHT

Thirty-seven thousand feet below me
the town barely exists. And yet
somewhere in that faint scatter of lights
a woman has just walked out behind her house,
worn by her day with kids. She stops on the patio,
lights a cigarette, flips the spent match
into the dark, looks up to the stars
and there I am, five miles above her eyes

curious traveller, stranger who might
have been lover, part of this bond
of just-visible lights: she,
drawn for a moment to this moving star,
transported to her most intimate fantasy;
me, reaching down to touch,
touch with words the darkness,
her night, this small moment.

## ALEXANDRA

Twenty years forgetting can
never wipe our memories clean.

Newpapers forget. Telecasts can
not outlive each day's new killings.

The beauty contest you won is forgotten.
The patients you nursed are well, or dead.

The river grasses no longer hear
the screaming in your blood.

The police have found new mysteries,
new bloodlettings, new victims.

But somewhere a tormented man
sits in darkness of his own,

and no river can wash from his mind
the slow flow of your dying.

He can not twist his hands enough
to wipe the feel of your flesh away.

Each day your face will grow
younger in his album of dark recall

until the day he will believe
it love and must tell all.

# THE HISTORY OF CHINA

Going back several thousand years in Chinese history
through a maze of ancient wisdom, back
in time so remote and distant
there can be no focus on friends,
three poets in a country
where history is a story of grandfathers
and seventy centuries lies beyond
the boundaries of minds.

My friends are caught in a frenzy of images:
they are writing poems about China.
One has visited the country and roots
poems in the fertile soil of touch and dream,
a landscape he may never see again,
except as ragged moths of memory drawn
against the window pane, against the night.
The other moves through remembered pages
read of Chinese sailors, emigrants who left
precarious certainties of home to seek
unknown familiarities of distant shores.
The eyes of my friends are vigilant pools
where strange fish swim, delicate as silk
stitched in the embroidery of remembrance.

I am the curious third of this tentative bond
who shambles through the silences of the two
who are intent to draw to them the voices
that may speak to them today, somewhere
down this promenade of Oriental time. Perhaps
these same voices that sing in their ears
will have some least words to whisper to me.

# WOOD MOUNTAIN OCTOBER

Subtleness of October sun. Coulees aflame.
Wind smells winter. Trees draw into themselves.

Three mule deer. Against a fading hillside.
A ring of stones. Forgotten stories.

This empty homestead. A lone spruce.
Memories in other minds, distant places.

Sun slant on stubble. Harvest aftermath.
Mallards feeding, heads green as spring.

Geese. Etched lines on sky. Autumn's cliché.
Cock pheasant on the road. Brilliant arrogance.

The beauty in this land. Summer's death.
We believe in this. The wonder of the seed.

# HOOKERS OF ST. JOHN'S

Below street level in the Seabreeze lounge
seamen reel in from the world's boats,
fishermen cast up from western Europe,
from Asia and from South America,
their ships at anchor a block or so away.

Inside the Seabreeze several idle whores
exchange tidbits about the latest ship.
Hookers like gulls await each new crew,
their lines ready for sea-weary men.
They ply their nets in every language,
in wordless language, unwritten messages
to men who need women. They are universal,
these fishers of the Seabreeze,
part of the city like the gulls.
They cry out their welcome, cast out lines
to each new ship. Their perfume rides
the waves of cigarette smoke, the harbour smell.

# GOLDFISH AND BUMBLEBEES

Sitting at a little restaurant table, confident
in his home territory, the poet
chooses his poems from early work,
opens his world to us here.

Sometimes he is the goldfish
and we, gawkers, peer through glass.
The image is clear as the water
he glides through with natural ease.

Sometimes he is the bumblebee,
wrapped in the flower's close,
locked into love's last bloom
as winter stills the world of bees.

His singing swims and buzzes
over and around and through
us all, murmurs of Dickinson
and MacEwen, Pound and Yeats.

Closer and closer we are drawn
into a nectared world of words,
sounds that flash and flutter
through glass and petals of poems.

Driving to Esterhazy on this last day
in March I have passed from spring
showers to sunshine,
and now near Lanigan the old
seasonal struggle comes skidding into focus.
I am caught in a prairie blizzard,
fighting snow driven by a northwest wind,
steering with two-handed tentativeness
on this treacherous highway to spring.

And through the slanting snow
just above the road ahead I see
two Canada geese struggle, ragged
against the bite of wind.
Their plaintive cries carry
the breath of spring,
push dogged winter north.

## MORNING OF HOAR FROST

This morning hoar frost
rims the outer world, trees
rimed, cold beauty.

A few leaves still
tremble in their dance
on the pale Griffin poplar.

This backyard world once more
a snapshot of the past,
a reminder of other frost:

the child I was, city-born,
learning winter in Saskatchewan
at ten on a prairie farm;

this same frost feathered
aspen groves like snow,
and the world was a frozen sea.

My patient uncle explained
the difference between snow
and this lacework of frost.

And now that this same trim
of white has won over my hair
with its own wintry reminder

these fragile frost-work mornings
sing a pale and delicate song.
Time pauses on the edge of rime.

# GIRL IN THE BLACK LOUNGE CHAIR

Waiting for my night class to begin,
smoking that one last cigarette,
I notice the girl
curled in the black lounge chair
reading a letter, lost
to everything around her.

Her eyebrows arch suddenly.
Her lips move in silence, break
into a momentary smile, then
she closes the letter slowly,
touches it lightly to her lips,
returns it to the envelope.

For a moment her eyes touch mine.

I go to my class troubled:
a young girl, her smile, a message,
these small moments, so many
letters I should have written.

## TORONTO STREET SCENE

The two of them walk
Yonge Street in rain.
Unhappy pair, her face
wears a mist of hurt;
his is a dark storm.
Step by step they stride
in practised tandem.
Her sorrow tilts an umbrella
over his anger, not as
a shield or a balm,
but because she would
do no less, and he
would do no more.

## BACKYARD MOMENT
(for Ray Souster)

The robin has just settled
into the birdbath and now
cocks its head at me
expectantly.

                Out of habit,
family man that I am,
I turn my eyes away
discreetly.

## SHELLING PEAS

In the desert heat of Saskatchewan August
like exhausted dancers peas wilt by mid-day;
you must rise in the early morning to pick
the plump pods at their peak of freshness.

In the shade you sit with three containers:
the basket of peas, waiting to be depearled,
the smaller bucket for the rattle of peas,
the waste container for the emptied pods.
You take care in the placement of the three —
eliminate wasted movement, position each
to suit your handedness, minimize the time
between the plucking of the fresh pod
and expelling of the spent shell.

Your thumbnail becomes an oyster knife
to pry the shell, the thumb slides inside
the violated lips and thrums the gems
into the bucket in a green dance of hail;
the other hand flips the husks away.
In seconds it is a familiar act,
new as spring, ageless as love:
slit of thumbnail, crack of entry,
chorus of peas, snap of discards.
You slip easily into this harvest ritual,
become one with a million others
who ply this same rite of summer.

There is no boredom here in repetition.
Each pod is its own mystery, its own small world.
And you become the eternal peasant, held
in abounding fascination with living things.

You now become a mere extension
of something you sense but can not fully know:
why this ritual courses small, almost imperceptible
tremors through the nerves and sinews of the arm
to warm the thumb and fingers with old messages.
You lapse into the easy movement of the hands
with a satisfaction that lies just below
the skin of consciousness like tiny emeralds
singing their green notes in mid-summer dance.
In the coolness of early morning you turn
the seasons between your thumb and fingers
and hold the rain in your hands.

80 03

*from* STALKING PLACE:
POEMS BEYOND BORDERS

DOZER MAN AND THE SHAMAN

Baffin Island. Brilliant with summer sun.
Flower-bursts flood the short season,
hillsides flaunt their colours.
Sunday afternoon. Work at a rare standstill.
Dozer man on a day of rest
wanders through incredible hues of Arctic
summer, a man drunk on landscape.
He tops a rise, sees below him
Inuit gathered in a natural amphitheatre.

One man clearly leads his people
in some ceremony — a shaman, perhaps
an invocation of the sun. Dozer man watches
the ritual to its end. He is silent.
The shaman's incantations in a language
he does not understand provoke a desire
in dozer man to descend the hill,
to speak with this man. He does not know
the words he wants to say; he does not know
whether the shaman will speak to him.
But the need intensifies as he sees, listens.

The ceremony over, the dozer man moves
down the slope, moves like a dreamer
through his own dreamscape. The Inuit disperse,
except for the shaman who waits
as if the meeting were prearranged.
The dozer man seethes with questions
that swirl like sandflies around his head.
He offers the shaman his name, seeks words
to shape the mysteries he has witnessed,
the turmoil set free inside him.

Before the first question can bubble to his lips
the shaman raises his hand, silences the dozer man.
The shaman's eyes hold this stranger
who has come a thousand miles and more
to this chance encounter in another world.
Here in the vivid intenseness of Baffin summer
the dozer man is held in silence until
the shaman speaks his words:

> *I can say only this to you*
> *and you must hear me well.*
> *You must kill your god.*
> *Only then can you be free.*

As if the question were asked, the shaman adds:

> *When the time comes, you will know.*

The dozer man is befuddled. His tongue
becomes a lump of soapstone in his mouth.
These words have no meaning for him.
He does not know he is not free.

Questions uncork his tongue, words
pour forth. Again the shaman raises his hand.
He repeats his admonition, word for word.
Then turns and walks away.

The dozer man is deserted, mystified.
His eyes become the eyes of a snowy owl,
his wonder the colour of Arctic summer.

Christmas. Holiday time for dozer man.
Arctic islands a distant summer memory.
In the Quebec village of his grandfather
dozer man relaxes into nightly rounds
to relatives — drink and talk, music and song
spin night into morning. In the house
of his grandfather, now his mother's,
the night of the party, he walks outside
into the cold to piss, moonlight
a splash of silver across the snow,
stands alone under a flashing of stars.
And hears the owl.

The bird hoots. Very close.
He peers up. There in a sprawling maple
he sees it: a large snowy owl.
He knows this bird well, his Arctic years.
*Strange*, he muses. He grew up here
and never saw such a great white owl
until his dozer took him north.
*Has this owl followed him home?*
Dozer man feels uneasiness slide
through his veins, disquiet gnaw him.
The shaman's words return:

> *You must kill your god.*
> *Only then can you be free.*

Dozer man decides. He returns to the house
and brings back his grandfather's .22 rifle.
When the owl falls at his shot
he feels exhilaration. He has never
killed an owl before, never wanted to.

Next day the villagers come,
one by one to see the great white owl.
No one can recall such a bird.
For a time there are no more
shaman voices in dozer man's head.
He may even believe that he is free.

ᏆᎦ ᏉᎦ

# *from* AIR CANADA OWLS

## STREET SWEEPERS' NOCTURNE

3:30 a.m. Through the hotel window
from the street below the sounds intrude,

intrude upon the restless sleep we toss in:
unfamiliar bed, another time our blood rejects.

I stand at the window. Down the Kaiserstrasse
a truck sprays the sidewalks with water;

street sweepers follow with their brooms.
Insomniacs sweep away the night.

Their heavy-bristled thrusts, this way and that,
ready Frankfurt's face for our tomorrow.

Refuse of the daytime strews the sidewalk
world of night and now the sweepers come,

silent, but for the bristled swish that marks
their passing and the cobbled street lies still.

Then Frankfurt will rise to business schemes
while sweepers drop into their tidy dreams.

## INCIDENT IN THUNDER BAY

The K-Mart does not permit its cashiers
to give out change for a dollar. This infuriates
me. My wife wants to make a long distance call
and between us we haven't a dollar's change.

In the store rotunda where the pay phones are
I vent my anger, my frustration, wave my dollar bill
like a political manifesto. I am about to launch
my favourite monologue — a rote tirade against
the utter stupidity of bureaucratic chainstores
when . . .
a young woman, leaving, pushing a stroller,
hears my harangue, fears for her child
in the presence of such verbal contamination,
stops, digs in her purse, offers me her change.
She thrusts eighty-five cents at me. I hand
her the dollar. She refuses. But I insist.
Her refusal is even more adamant. A crowd gathers.
Her stubbornness rivals that of Grandfather Sorestad
who built an unenvied reputation for bull-headedness.
(Of course, I don't tell her this.) I try instead
to stuff my dollar bill in her kid's mouth.
But the same streak seems to run in the kid
and the woman's look tells me she is convinced
she's in the presence of a certified lunatic.

In the end, it turns out we didn't need the change.
My wife, by this time realizing the folly
of expecting me to get a dollar's change
without creating a scene, charged the call.
So I am left with a dollar bill in one hand
and eighty-five cents in the other, wondering
what kind of story this good samaritan
will tell her husband when he gets home.

## ALL THE MOTHERS IN THE WEST BUT MINE
## ARE FLYING TO TORONTO

I am surrounded, front and back
and to the side by a bevy of young mothers
and small children. The urchins take turns
erupting into howls, spontaneous duets or trios.
The mothers soothe, soothe in the ageless
language of mothers, tenderest of guiles.

One child is pacified, then another, until
the aircraft cabin almost becomes a triumph
of motherhood. But then one two-year old
with a shriek that could split atoms
rejects all endearments and bribery. He
will have his way, and we will all become
accomplices to his mother's growing desperation.
The others take the cue. An infant conspiracy
against their mothers, who boarded this flight
with only minor trepidation, but will deplane
as tearful wrecks, each certain forever that it was
the other child, the other mother, that invoked
this maddened mob of intractable howlers.

We are still an hour and a half from Toronto
and already my hands are beginning to quiver.
I have forgotten what it was like to pace
the midnight floor with a fretful child.
The man next to me just gulped a double scotch.
I can hear his silent vows of bachelorhood.

All the mothers in the west but mine
are enroute to Toronto with their squalling gems
and I have this feeling that I am being punished
for something I can't remember doing or saying
either to my mother or my own children.
But should this caterwaul of lungs persist
I know, O how I know, I shall remember.

If I were a painter I would
have been tempted, there and then
to stop, set up easel and canvas,
gather oils and brushes and palette,
and capture you as you slept.

Slumped in your chair
in the midst of the pedestrian mall,
oblivious to the multitude that streamed
on every side of you, the ruckus
of a hundred languages or more
completely voided as you dreamed . . .

      perhaps of that younger
      child stepping light-footed
      through dark forests, or
      clambering mountain paths
      to unspeakable brilliance
      of alpine heights
      snow-capped sky.

I would have wanted to lock
forever into configurations of pigment
the delicious slouch of your body
as it slid from September afternoon
into ageless wonder of dreams,
to have kept the curve and droop
of that meerschaum pipe
in your moustached mouth
for all time.

COWBOY CHRIST
(for Tony Clark)


In Paris, Texas, Christ rises above
the final rest of Willet Babcock.
The long-dead rancher is well anchored
for fierce winds. He cares little

about the three of us, drawn here
not for prayers over Babcock's bones,
but to stare, as we do now, up
at this sculpted Christ astride

Babcock's massive headstone
that derricks twenty feet against
the wintry Texas sky, His shoulder
against the cross, flowing robe

to His feet. We are poets all, two
fled south from a frozen country
to follow our Texas colleague here,
to scuff the stoney path to Babcock

though the pebbles we dislodge above
are bootless to his ears as we
assume the perfect vantage point to see
beneath the robe of Jesus His left foot,

His cowboy boot. Why shouldn't I believe
that in Texas even He would wear boots?
For the moment we are silent as Babcock,
gathered here around the feet of Christ.

# FOUR AIRPORTS IN LATE NOVEMBER

Calgary. Sun-slant cracks the snow clouds.
An oil donkey beside the runway, metal head
slow rocking, the darkness of crude below.

Great Falls. Snow-pellets shot from the mountains.
Beside the runway two small hares, not yet white,
caught in a downwind dash by early winter.

Salt Lake City. Airliners stacked in slow circles.
A final swoop to the Utah flats in dimming light
and a glide to the hubbub of terminal madness.

El Paso. Following the light-strewn Rio Grande
and over the Franklin Mountain darkness to where
west Texas bridges old Mexico at Juarez.

## PICKING CHERRIES IN THE OKANAGAN

The season is almost over, most trees
already stripped. The crop has been
forgettable — too much rain has swelled
and split the fruit. Roadside stands offer
cut rates on the last bloated cherries.

A rough sign: CHERRIES U-PICK.
We wheel from the road to an orchard
and a grizzled farmer takes us to the last
unpicked cherry tree in his grove.
He shows us how to pull the stems back
towards the tree so as not to damage
the buds beneath: the beginnings in place
already for next year's crop. Pails in hand
we ascend ladders he arranges out of July sun
into coolness of upper branches, quiet shade,
to pluck the dark fruit. The season's
final cherries wait like gems
before our eager fingers. In a world
of computerized commerce we have climbed
to the simple excitement of a primal rite.

While the sweet cherries rise in our pails
the farmer stands below, watches, explains
how unseasonal rains ruined the Valley crop,
how his orchard was one of few spared. His eyes,
upturned, inspect the efficiency of our job,
while his busy mind calculates how many
pounds at fifty cents a pound
our imperfect fingers can spin to gold for him.

From my perch I glance down, see him
as his cherries must, here as the last
ruby flicker fades back into his upturned eyes.

Next week his eyes will be peaches.

The cigar and sports shirt might suggest it,
but the voice confirms where he's from:

> *Look at the pollution from those factories!*
> *They'd never git away with that in Pennsylvania.*

We stand in the aisle and smoke, watch factories
and land slip by as the train rolls northwest
from Paris to the Normandy seacoast.

> *Now if they hired me I'd clean up this mess*
> *and set them straight in no time at all.*

He's self-made president, made his fortune
specializing in hazardous waste disposal.

> *They say they're ahead of us,*
> *but they're really behind us, I figure.*
> *They'd never allow this in Pennsylvania.*

His voice clangs with absolute conviction.

I remind him of the acid rain in Canada —
the dying forests of Ontario and Quebec,
the pollution of the Great Lakes, toxic
chemicals seeping into the Niagara River
from New York wastes and factories. But he
has never heard of these things; his voice
takes on an edge of skepticism as he slides
into the safety of homefield advantage:

> *It would never happen in Pennsylvania!*

Later as we roll through the dark hills of Normandy
through lush forests and grassy pastures, he says:

*There's a whole lot of good American blood*
    *in them hills.*
                    Unshakable, unmistakable pride.

I tell him about all the Canadian troops who fought
their way through the hell that was Normandy beaches,
how one Canadian beach-head and the thrust inland
that followed helped save two embattled American
landing forces pinned down on the lead-strafed beach.

He didn't know Canadians were even involved,
says his history classes never mentioned it at all.
The tone of his voice as good as calls me liar.

"My uncle died there on those beaches,
you pompous ass," I want to say. But instead,
I tell him, *I want to see my uncle's grave.*
*He died here in Normandy too. That's why I'm*
*on this train. I want to find his grave,*
*maybe try to understand why he died.*
And then I can't resist adding:
*It's too bad he died there just for us Canadians.*

# AMSTERDAM DOG WALKER

Along the canal she came, the young woman
drawn on a spider web of leashes by seven dogs,

seven multi-sized mutts trotting in strange sync
along the canal path in canine unconcern.

When one dog stopped to squat or lift a leg
the other six all automatically dallied;

some sank on haunches, others stood,
but all were trained to treat each stop

as an inalienable right of dogdom. Each
no doubt having its turn to pick and choose

the spot to sniff or snuffle. And the woman
strolled behind, silent and content, holding

the reins of this peculiar everyday procession;
leader or follower, she was vital to the group.

Long after they had passed and disappeared beyond
the canal's curving course, it occurred to me:

it was a silent entourage. Not one yip or yap,
nor growl nor grumble; not one word of admonition

or impatience from her who walked behind. Silent
and uncanny, this promenade of woman and dogs

who knew each other's needs, had made this stroll
so often now there was no need for words,

except the subtle, silent language of the links
of living leash that bound them each to each.

## THE GEORGIA HOTEL, VANCOUVER

Inside the Georgia businessmen in hard shell
tailor-made three-piece respect chatter blue chips.

On Hornby Street a woman redolent with rental love
leans, her dark mascaraed eyes pin-pricks of forgetting.

Over candled linen clatter legs of Alaskan crab.
On the sidewalk the woman waits, scarlet claws impatient.

# WHATEVER HAPPENED TO JANE JAYROE?

In Laverne, Oklahoma, the people wait,
await the return of their queen.

We drive beneath the banner hanging
over Main Street, the banner that proclaims
Laverne as "Home of Jane Jayroe". It intimates
how America showered Jane with kisses
that day they placed the crown on her head,
the teary-eyed Miss America of 1967.

The pride is still here in Laverne:
the banner must be newly done each spring
as Lavernians relive the day two decades past.

*But what of Jane Jayroe, where is she?*
*Whatever becomes of all the Jayroes?*
*Do they marry football heroes, grow fat,*
*become sippers of afternoon vodka,*
*have babies who will become quarterbacks*
*or movie queens? Do they settle for a few*
*years of magazine covers, swimsuit ads*
*before younger Miss Americas replace them?*
*Do they become mistresses for movie moguls*
*or state senators? Talk show hosts or hookers?*
*Whatever happened to Jane Jayroe?*
*Did she abandon Laverne forever in 1967?*

Jane Jayroe, wherever you are, come back.
Come home to Laverne, Oklahoma.
The banner shouts, the folks grow restless,
the news two decades old. Crowsfeet
may have lined your lovely face, Jane,
but in Laverne, Oklahoma, it doesn't matter.
In Laverne the people wait, Jane.
They wait for you.

# NIGHT FLIGHTS

I look up tonight and watch a bank of cloud
slink across the Hunter and the chase,
watch another light move against the slow
flow of clouds, a night jet at 35,000 feet
caught between the skin of earth
and the infiniteness of stars
slashing the night sky with its urgency
pressing unknown people to their commitments.

I have taken night flights like this,
have flashed across your darkness, a moving star.
I remember one late night flight from Vancouver:
a young woman and two small fretful children,
all three jaded by a full day of airports.
I took one of the youngsters on my knee
and my seatmate, a logger, took the other
so the young mother could catch a needed nap.

There is a special eeriness about night flights
when the world outside your window is a void
and you can't believe that you are etching
an unseen vapour trail against the darkness
that you are higher than the highest falcon
swifter than the fastest hunter of the sky
that you are a curious light in someone's night.

Yes, I have taken night flights and tonight
watching this point of light above me
on its relentless traverse of the dark, I wonder:

*Who is up there, looking down from some window?*
*Has someone up there spotted Saskatoon just now*
*through a break in the clouds, noticed the spatter*
*of lights and wondered if anyone below was watching?*
*Perhaps another poet is up there, coming or going*
*from another reading, pen in hand, filling time*
*roughing out lines about night flights?*

༄ ༄

*from* WEST INTO NIGHT

EARLY MORNING SUN

1.

Two grain elevators
pry the reluctant
sun up from
the horizon
and slowly,
slowly raise it
to their shoulders.

2.

I was wrong — again.
There were three
elevators and the sun
was levered up
the sky by two
while the foreman
stood by and watched.

## GRANDFATHERS

I pick up my grandson
and hoist his sturdy body
to ride in the clasp of my arm.
How good it feels.

I remember holding two sons,
one under each arm, nothing
to numb the arm and shoulder
or cause the back to stiffen
in this martial posture.
My arm weakens.

I wish I could remember
my own grandfathers holding me
like this. Did either
ever snatch me up to ride
atop his shoulders, tiny cowboy,
legs around his neck, hands
clinging to his head
as to a pommel horn,
then take me off alone,
just grandfather and grandson,
off to see red strawberries
or new kittens in the barn?

Grandfathers hold us.
Through time and dreams they
raise us up toward that place
where an arm surrounds us
in endless memory.

# TUNNELS

When they entered the darkness
their headlights were futile gestures.

He was several years into his eighties
and she a few years younger. Tunnels

through mountains were an unknown terror
they broached on faith alone. His eyes,

enfeebled by age, books and grain dust
could not adjust to the absence of light;

her voice guided his hands on the wheel,
led them from day through night to day.

In his eighty-fifth year he crumpled
with a stroke that left his memory

a highway grid fraught with tunnels
on every road. Now in the nursing home

she talks with him each day, her voice
his eyes still, still the guide that steers

him through the past, through memories
she had not even shared. His hands still

cling to the steering wheel as she speaks,
as she leads them surely down the road.

They are both driving through the dark;
moving surely to a brilliance of light.

## THE SONG OF MOUNT RUNDLE
(for Robert Sinclair)


He is painting the song that he hears
in that moment when rock sheers sky,

when the sun relaxes its grip on the day
and evening brushes its delicate hues.

The song source is deep as memory is old,
and colours are yet to be seen;

but the song leaps to the gathering sky
and climbs where all songs become one,

where the ageless song of the mountain
merges with the spirit-dance of stars.

He is painting the song that he hears
in the moment his brush touches paper,

and the strokes are notes that sing
the multi-tinted movement of the night

meeting day. Rock and sky, sun and star
sing in his head, sing in his eyes,

sing the song through his fingers dancing,
dancing the song down from the stars

and the sun, down where rock meets sky.
He is dancing the song down to rest.

## ROCKY MOUNTAIN MORNING

The smell of the mountain
tumbles down into the trees
and first light splinters
through the pine-nailed path.

Three deer graze a patch
of new green growth, raise
their heads to watch me pass.
Mountain morning walks in me.

## MOMENTS FROM THE PAST

It happened coming home from a dance
and we sat, strangers in a crowded backseat,
caught up in the aftermath, the giddy buzz
of just another Saturday night dance.

A sudden swerve of the car brought
your head to rest upon my shoulder —
where it stayed. Something shared in silence.
A moment I thought time had buried.

# THE WELL

Deep in the aspens beside a creek
The well of my childhood still
Holds the purest water, sweet and cold.

My dreams still draw me there
To pump from the cool depth of days
Long past the essence of my youth,

So many days gone by. So many
Fleeting moments have I pulled
From the place that holds my past.

I dip from the watery dark
And spill the memories to my taste.
The creek flows away. Go slow.

Nights grow long. The well
Calls me to its aspen shade
To drink again the sweet chill

That sets the teeth aflame.
I must return. Let aspens grow.
Let me hear the creek's slow flow.

## AIDE MEMOIRE

The world begins and ends in memory;
what I remember is what I am.

Did that blade of grass I plucked
as a boy to vibrate with my breath

really burst the air with shrillness?
A remembered world holds truth

and realities far clearer than echoes.
In the cupped hands of remembrance

the thin green reed of what we are
trembles with a sound so rare.

GYPSY FIRE

Come to the light of this gypsy fire.
The leap of flame, crack of wood-burst,
sparks thrust from the fire's core
like satellites spun through the night:
these will hold us here. Come and become
one with this late night fire circle.

We will talk. Or we may lapse
into the long silence of fire-watching,
watching ourselves become the first
fire-fascinated people crouched
around the primal dancing flames.
We will read our history in firelight.

Look closely to the flicker and whirl.
Somewhere in the fire the child stares back,
all that you have been. All you've known.
Look closely. Each moment is there
lingering on the edges of the fire-dance.
Know yourself, if you would. Look again.

# HAWK WITH BROKEN WING

The bird whose wing
drags by its side
is now confined
to earth. It misses

the lift of air
currents carrying
it ever upward.
The heights.

Creature of air
it must return
to healing sky
to be renewed.

A crippled hawk
that flaps despair
on alien grass
will not survive.

One wing can never
thrust it to the sky.
The mending air can
never make it whole.

NIGHT SKY

It is enough to hold
a bouquet of diamond
flowers, to stand before
the night and reach
your fingers up to pluck
them from their garden,
to see them as your own,
to will them into daytime
bloom. That is enough.

It is enough to say
yes, I have held the stars,
felt their mystery touch
my fingers as I embraced
them only for a moment
and all the vessels of my arms
floated on a sea of night.
Yes, it is enough.

## MOON THOUGHTS

It might have been
something in the soft
flush of moonlight
as it slid cool
fingers through your hair

reminding me
                decades later
of you
        when moon thoughts
first crept across my mind.

# LATE SUMMER CROWS

Field upon field of wheat turns
in its cycle of green to gold
as I drive through summer's dying.

Above grain that sends waves
in slow measure shore to shore
a still sky glazed with sun.

Against this duo-toned day
erratic unexpected movement:
black rags on the sky, a shout of crows.

Harbingers of summer's decay, crows
read the season's cryptic message,
muster their numbers in the gathering gold.

Black flakes drift against August sun,
somber and sure as obituaries, sound
grave edicts across the sky.

# REDSTREAK MOUNTAIN MORNING

Windchimes hang silent and still
as in some distant memory of sound,

but birdsong cascades from conifers
and a woodpecker beaks percussion.

Grey sky rides the grim peaks above;
the distant Purcells are a faded wash.

Morning switchbacks down Redstreak
through insect whine and tree shiver

to where I sit, where I watch and listen
for the born-again wind to rouse the trees

and give the windchimes back its song.

## CAT IN MORNING

See how the distant
ages live
       in this
            soft tread
     this slow,
               deliberate
stalk;
      how many savage
kills
     ripple
         its sleek fur.

This cat lives
         on death.
Forget
      the lazy afternoon
comfort
      in its throaty
           purr.

The breast-torn
         bird
knows nothing
       of this sound.

It is morning
       now and
its careful
     step
      worries
the small
     of fur
       and feather.

The cat
       is stealth
moving
       through time,
its blood
       hot,
its belly
       empty.

The late October sun lies west,
a cold slide into the Arctic sea.

Seven miles below the world falls away.
Frozen twilight. Crust of Baffin Island.

Striations: rock and ice, rock and ice.
Cold half-light reaches up and up.

We move always west. There is sun again.
Sunrise that is illusion. Resurrection.

The coldness below is no illusion:
sun can not burn away this ice.

Ice speaks the language of long night.
West, you must always fly to night.

# THE OLD PLACE

*. . . all I want is a little time*
*to stand here a final time  some things*
*after all exist beyond the crowbar*
*and the sledge . . .*

*— William Kloefkorn*

There is something in us that denies change,
that wants the memory unaltered by time,
especially those places we have lived
and dwell still in reverie and dream.

In this old house I sit, look south
down the road I cycled as a youth,
the road I could not wait to take
to freedom, and all that I desired.

Now time has led me back this road,
not the first time, but each time
could be the last. In this house
all I want is to sit and be still,

look out through these same windows
as that distant child I was, imagining
the heroic roles he'd have to play.
I do not know just what I want to see —

perhaps those childhood horses trotting
up the hill, my father's car returning —
I only sense it is the being here,
looking out this window, that matters.

# MARBLES

Memories of childhood wheel and wheel —
small pebble moments spun from the turning
at random, sometimes caught in wakeful hours,
sometimes lost as dreams arc through sleep.
This small sphere that held that freckled kid
snapping and flicking marbles locked
in the poise of right thumb and forefinger
has spun with time to merge with other circles;
and the marbles of memory are more and more
in play as the child kneels to the game again,
eager to win that perfect marble, the one
that will acknowledge him within his code
as all he ever saw himself, or ever was.

## FOURTEEN

Whatever became of blue-eyed Jeannie
whose swelling breasts were magnetic fields
that seized our eyes like iron filings?

In our coltish play of bump and push
we teased and ran from knowing's edge,
ran like scolded pups from her mock-chiding.

That summer's sudden rounding of her body
caught us unprepared at fall's return;
the thrust of her newness thundered,
rolled our boyhood summers into the past,
triggered a new volcanic surge
that drove our nights to wonder.

## THE BEAUTY OF SILENCE

I think I am beginning to understand,
to know why it was you said

so little to me then, much preferred
to write a letter, send a book.

I too have lost the will to say
again and again what must be said.

I too know the beauty of silence,
know the need to speak that wars

with our desire to hear silence
say the things that we can not.

So many times I've looked into myself
and found your silence there, Father.

# TWO FISH, ONE MORNING

Late October, a cold morning,
we were driving home to the farm
from the city for the weekend:
*Why do I remember this now?*
*Why now, with you gone, the memory*
*like an empty place at a family dinner?*

"Let's stop at the lake and fish,"
you said; I argued for a warm bed.
But you persisted,
you often did, and we stopped there —
the pre-dawn chill, deserted shoreline,
the boats of summer now high and dry,
but for one; and we rowed out on the grey
slight chop as dawn shivered
with autumn frost. Offshore we anchored,
fumbled numb-fingered over tackle,
our backs hunched against the cold breeze.

All of this was thirty years ago:
two brothers, a whim you had that I
acceded to as brothers do. Remember
how the grey sky lightened
and the wind grew, made us huddle
on the floor of that old wooden rowboat,
our clothes unsuited to this wild notion?

We cast our chosen lures and cursed
our numb and gloveless hands
that didn't want to be here at all.
Then the first pike hit your lure so hard
it snapped you upright, almost pitched

you overboard; and you fought the fish
until it pounded on the floor beside us —
twelve pounds of fury, its sleek skin
curiously warm to my stiffened fingers.

Soon I too was fighting one, its sudden
strike setting my cold hands to work
as if fisherman's memory was energy
to fuel numb hands with fire. I too
reeled the large and vicious pike
(it could have been a deadringer for yours)
to the boat and you reached into the chill
water, hauled the fish in by the leader.

And we leaned against the sides,
kindled with excitement and laughter,
and stared at the two largest pike
we'd ever taken from these waters.
We fished no more that morning.

Nor ever again. It was the last time
we fished together, though I have since
dreamed many trips we should have taken,
as our lives pulled us separate ways.

But now, this sudden retrieval, this double
barb of memory: that day, when for a time
we were as one — a single fisherman,
hooked, sinew and bone, to a single fish —
one cold morning in October when
for a time there was no time at all
and we were either nothing or everything,
two brothers crazed with the wisdom of fools.

# THE MAN WHO WOULD BE A FISH

He loves the smooth glide
of water against his skin,
longs for the shape
of a trout. He wants to dart
into the deepest pools.

The silence of dark water
pleases him, where trout live
trouty lives without need
to wheedle or accuse.
He would forget words.

The man would be a fish
and lie in sun-dappled streams,
study the surface above.
The slightest nymphet ripple
would launch him open-mouthed

to swirl the water's skin
in a snap of jaws, a flash
of coloured flank. He would grow
old in a hookless world,
in an absence of words.

# THE RETURNING

Some days he recognizes her,
other days she is a stranger —
his wife this past quarter-century.

Yet she visits him often, seems content,
for reasons mostly unclear to him,
to sit beside him here in his room.

Some days he is a child of ten
wondering whether his father, dead
for seventy years now, is well.

This woman who is his second wife
has shared the last third of his life
and now, beginnings — the fragile past

as he creeps back to the womb.
A bittersweet sharing, this return.
She leaves the visit tired, confused.

It is this hard falling back
to childhood, each moment nearer when
sun and rain, star and stone are one.

## AN ABSENCE OF BIRDS

Summer is hot and dry. Not unusual.
The ambient sounds: wind in old elms,
grasshoppers buzz the daylight,
tractor, road and field sounds.
A chatter of sparrows in carraganas.
At night the long quaver of coyotes,
the yapping of foxes.

                           Something is missing.
Remembered sounds, no longer there.
Where is the soft call of mourning doves?
What happened to the nighthawk's cry
balancing on the margin of day and night?

The hamlet shrivels like droughted wheat.
Someone dies. Houses empty. Fewer mourners.
Fewer gardens echo sounds of spring,
fewer hoes at war with weeds.
Fewer pails of water from the well.
Ebbing sound.

An absence of birds is its own sadness:
each year another sound heard no more.
Who will restore the chorus
to what memory desires,
to what spirit demands?

ॐ ༄

*from* JAN LAKE SHARING

THE LAKE

The lake is a living thing — it moves,
trembles and shudders with the wind,
with the seasons, with the rain.

Shorelines, island and reefs — shapes
that shift in a glance, never identical.
At first everything appears the same,

but you learn to read the shore:
let this rockface, that crooked spruce
fix itself in your eye,
then in the space behind your eye.

Memory holds a lake alive, dreams
a lake into the blood's geography.

AUTOFOCUS

*Click.* This is the caught moment: the son holds
his mini-camera, focuses with care; he wants
to capture it all. His father holds the seven pound pike
stretched full-length. It glistens, even in the absence
of sun, posing for the take, its ancient predatory
appearance held there like history. *Click.*
The father's pride and pleasure — this event
he has come so far to find. In the background
the stern of the boat, the lake's dark water,
the spruce-spiked shoreline, the grey sky — all
recorded on film in this micro-second. *Click.*
The sound of the film moving no more audible
than the passing of this moment into memory.
Who will recall the slap of waves
against the boat, the sound of the wind
in the evergreen dark? The father places
the pike back into the water from which he has
taken it, holds it gently as the waves renew
its strength, the gills begin to move.
Father and son watch as the pike gathers itself
and with a sudden sweep of its tail
dives to darkness below.

## TO BUILD A FIRE

A man has built a fire. Against the odds,
against the sleet, the snow, the gusts
that want to have their way, that would
laugh at fires and those who build them.
The man who nurtured it to life has learned
the way of Woodland Crees, has found
tindery firestart: tiny spruce twigs,
their needles brown and sere as parchment.
He has coaxed the flames to life, here,
outside our cabin, so we may sit together,
watch the flames as darkness claims our day,
so we may drink our coffee and allow
this warmth to hold us, feel the heat
slide up our legs, into our hands,
warm ourselves in this closeness. The man
beside me has come two thousand miles
to build this memory.

## THE PEOPLE

The Crees from Pelican Narrows are a constant presence,
an inescapable reminder that this is their summer home,
that before this Lodge, this fishing camp, there were
only the People and their summer home. They move through
camp, pass among us, the men as guides, women as domestics,
filleters of fish. Often they move in silence, a muteness
that speaks its own meaning. They are the history of this
lake. But we too must claim our own small chronicles.

Sometimes it is the Cree children who are among us: their
raucous shouts and cries like feeding gulls remind us of
children everywhere, of the children we were and still are,
inheritors of this history with our presence. And the
Cree encampment, unseen back among the dark spruce, is
yet another reminder of who they are, who we are.

80 03

*from* BIRCHBARK MEDITATIONS

NOTCHES

As my friend slides the knife
from the sheath belted to his waist

and carves another walleye notch
on the wooden bench seat of the boat,

I think of notches carved —
so many, large and small, to bring

us to this moment on Jan —
initials, hearts in treebark,

cryptic boredom notes etched
on old schooldesk tops, juvenile

messages scratched with would-be
wit in college toilet cubicles,

the notches of personal history
intermingled with those deadly

chronicled ones — on Colt .45s
or Sioux war bows or Bowie knives.

For history brings us here, friend,
an endless trail of notches;

the knife was born to your hand,
the sheath part of your skin;

and you, like me, the sum of all
the notches we have carved.

## FIRST LIGHT

Softest is the first light
that strokes the dark lake,
untouched yet by wind, just
the slow, silent caress of dawn.

ଧ ଔ

*from* ICONS OF FLESH

FIRST GREENING

I am back in the land of my youth
and the aspen woods are awash
with a pale watercolour green
that rekindles memory each May.

It is the right time to be here.
This gathering green is chlorophyl
for the mind and spirit, reminds us
that memory is reborn each time

we witness the ageless newness
of another spring. I walk through
trembling aspens into childhood,
to the first greening of the heart.

They are mustered in the lounge for me,
a dozen veterans, legions of memories on stiff legs,
by the C.O., a single-minded woman devoted
to program some interest into their dying.

She introduces me and I read to them — or try.
One silver-haired Vimy vet in fitful doze
snaps upright like a sentry caught napping.
Others stare past me to distant fields . . .

I read humorous poems into maimed silence
profound as the aftermath of battle. I try
poems about old-timers, homesteaders — read
with the inspired passion of third generation.

My poems fall on the floor among us
like dud grenades, wounding no one. I try
pub poems and finally one vet stirs,
announces loudly he is going to the john.

"Does anyone have any questions?" I implore,
prepared for another barrage of silence
and the ignominy of my imminent retreat.
The Vimy warrior finally breaches the hush

we've wrapped ourselves in. "Have you ever
been to the pub in St. Albert?" he asks.
"St. Albert, in Alberta? No, I can't say
I've ever been in the pub in St. Albert."

"Well, you should. Then you can write a poem
about it. My daughter lives in St. Albert.
I would really like to visit her, you know.
I haven't seen my daughter in a long time."

Then another veteran stirs and fixes me
with a bayonet stare, coughs, and rasps,
"If I told you about me and Billy in France
you could write a whole book of poems about it!"

The white-haired dozer bolts awake and thumps
his cane twice on the floor for attention.
"By God," he quavers, "those were good poems.
I myself once wrote poems . . . to my wife . . .

"when she was still alive . . . " his voice retreats.
Then, "Read us a poem about veterans," he suggests.
"I haven't written one yet. But I will.
And furthermore, you'll be in my poem," I say.

So this poem is for him, though he'll never read it.
He never got to make that visit to St. Albert either.

## POEMFISHING

It is the right weather for poems:
gentle drizzle spins the morning grey
and no sunglints will strike
the monofilament we cast
across chill water.

Some days poems lie deep
and will not rise to the lure
no matter the artful cast
and skill of retrieve,
no matter that we hold
our breath and will
the sudden rush of poem to line.

Today I am archetypal fisherman,
intent on the moment, alert
to signals from below the surface.
The rod bends, a poem has taken hold.

## A FISHING STORY

We three stand side by side
along the sandy shore of the river,
fishing rods in hand —
my eldest son, my grandson,
not yet five, and me.
We cast our lures into the water.
Though the youngest has not
yet mastered the casting skills
he, too, is fisherman this day.

His lack of skill does not matter
because he is here with us and we
are three generations of fishermen
here on the pretext of fish.
In truth we have come here to share:
this splendid watercolour sunset,
two grebes diving and resurfacing
just beyond our casts, but most of all
this time together, the three of us.

And I wonder: will my grandson
remember this, years from now when
he has grandsons of his own? Will he
recall with pleasure some moment past
when he was one of three generations,
three anglers in the fading light
waiting for a fish to strike?

BEFORE YOU SPEAK

You should know this about me:
that I am thought to be
neither vengeful,
nor spiteful,
nor mean-spirited,
not even trigger-tempered;

but know this also:
all the noted killers
of the Old West who
spoke with lead syllables
the harsh eloquence
of Colt .45s,

all of them, claims this
source I'm reading now,
yes, all of them,
without exception,
had blue eyes,
or grey eyes,
or blue-grey eyes
(the deadliest of all)

exactly like mine.

# THE MAN WHO SHOT THE SQUIRREL

He shot the red squirrel in early morning,
a first act to assert his place in the day.

He says the squirrel woke him with its chatter
and besides, it was a destructive creature.

I wondered just what it might have been of his
this squirrel destroyed, but knew his answer

was not a motive at all; it was proprietorial:
nature impinging on his own space must give way.

First generation born to a land of immigrants,
he still views any landscape as real estate

to be owned, not an environment to be shared
with other living things. The squirrel knew

nothing of this European-born thinking;
it hustled with an innate animal knowledge

of shortening days and the need to secure food.
Our rights do not extend to squirrels.

# TORNADO WARNING

A funnel cloud looms
on our horizon, whirls
rapidly toward us:
*take necessary precautions.*

Perhaps I might have held back
instead of lashing out as I did.

The sky darkens. In this
stillness before the storm,
an oppressive silence stifles.

Words, once spoken,
irretrievable as hailstones.

Even songbirds fall mute
before the tornado's approach:
a warning ignored at our peril.

## MY FATHER'S HOUSE

My father built just one house —
a small bungalow in Burnaby.
He spiked his dreams in each fir stud,
read our futures in the bubbles
of the spirit level as he measured
each board to precision. I think
he told me what a wonderful thing
it was to build your own house.
We lived there just three years
and when we moved Father built no more.

I am no carpenter, but sometimes
I dream of that other house
he sought to build but never did.

After the move we lived in others' houses,
Father never truly content, as if
in selling the little house on Georgia Street
he'd dealt away something of himself.
But he kept his carpenter's toolbox
and his dream of the house he'd someday build.

He must have told me of his dream,
but I was fifteen, a bit off plumb,
my own spirits bubbling with vague blueprints
of freedom and adventure and escape.
Once I'd left Father sometimes wrote me.
I no longer have the letters,
but I remember how little he wrote of himself,
how much he was concerned about what I'd do?
Typical father-to-son letters? I suppose,
no doubt filled with good advice —

of which I might even have used a tad.
He never mentioned houses, but I know now
he was building again, building a house
to withstand time, building the only way
he could, as the carpenter in each of us must.

THINKING FOR TRACY

You were a star
that flashed across our nights,
too brief your dance.
In day's harsh light
all laughter dies.

Only part of you
was ever with us
and will remain
though you are gone.
The silent hurt you
left to us, this memory.

No words can free the pain.

## THE MATTER OF POETIC DISCOURSE
(for Peter)

My friend and I are poets, which means
that most of our time together we argue,
agree about little, except that we
are friends, or that the time is right
to have a beer. Our wives have learned
that when we shout *Bullshit!* at each other
we are not about to trade punches
as some illogical outcome of discourse.

After all, we are poets, irrational as hell
and will never come to blows, no matter
how many times either may disparage
the other's notion. This verbal posturing
is just a ruse, nothing more; we know
the importance of an image in our line
of work, spend hours preparing our faces
to meet others. We are both right,
though I always assert my seniority
and consequent accumulation of literary
street-smarts as empirical proof that I
am right more often. We bicker out of love,
of course, though our wives have known this
longer than we. Like true friends we shout
our animated theories at each other.
Why would we sully such a friendship
by ever coming to an agreement?

(When my friend reads this he will
insist I have it wrong, again,
and I'll know then it is true,
though out of love I'll alter words,
shift a few lines to convince him
he's right and nothing is changed.)

# MOUNTAIN MORELS

From the charred ruins spring morels,
gems among mushrooms. Penile fungi lunge
erect to sunlight from the blackness
of last year's fire up Brewster Creek.

Gingerly I step between tree corpses
scorched black by flames, try to steer
among charcoal trunks that loom stark
around me like totem poles of coal.

A score of paces away my wife stitches
her own seam against the ravaged slope;
her eyes like mine dart across dark
ashes for the spongy fungus thrusts.

We fill a woven basket with morels,
goat-foot horizontal to the mountainside,
the only cost our clothes besmudged in black
and clamour like children over our trove.

We gather to ourselves these delights:
a gourmet mushroom feast, small treasures,
small moments. Today from fire's despair
we salvage this harmony of morels.

# WE NEED THESE SILENCES

the spaces that lie
between moments of sharing,
those times when it is
enough to feel the presence
of the other, the knowing
that this silence, too
is a gift;

the silence of the mountains
or the dark forest,
or the plains at night,
reaching out to touch
some part of us
that craves time alone;

the moments before sleep
or after waking, when the world
rises or falls into order,
finds shape and meaning
of its own.

We need these silences
as we need the words
we must first learn to say
and then forget
as we come to know
silence.

## TURNING A NEW LEAF

Would you see this leaf I hold
as green, pale as the first flush

of spring? Or would you say
that this is death I hand you

and even now decay sets in?
I would speak of tiny wonders,

these mysteries reborn each day
to hold the mind and heart in awe.

May I offer you this leaf again?

# WOMAN MOURNING

This woman who has mourned
her husband's death two decades
now lives in fear of Nazis
in her memories of occupation
of her homeland when she went
underground to resist;
she survived to this prairie town
to live in the isolation of fear
until her grief became grotesque.

She resists the medicines that would
lift her from this long depression:
there are stormtrooper smiles
on the faces of her doctors.

She mourns the passing of all things;
her fearsome youth, her children
with their elsewhere lives,
the house she wrapped about her
now an empty dream, and most of all,
the man who brought her here
then left her to her fears.

In the dark cave of mad voices
she seeks the truth. Sometimes she
hears a small girl's glad laughter,
a foreign sound.

UNWANTED WINGS
(for John V. Hicks)

A white table
pristine
on a cedar deck,
fresh and agleam,
but quite relaxed
among four companion
chairs in summer sun.

Look closer:
the purity of white
is dark-dappled
with unwanted
motion on its
milky surface —
a dozen flies.

## WAITING FOR THE DEER

I am waiting for the deer to come
down from the mountain forests
to feed on new grass where I wait.

I am waiting for the softening light
of eve to beckon them to move.
I am waiting here, waiting for the deer.

I know that certain way they move:
they glide, pale ghosts among the trees.
You can miss them if you only turn your head.

I'm waiting for the deer to come.
I tell you, I refuse to blink an eye;
I will not miss them, I say again to you.

I am waiting for the deer to come
and after they have passed and all is still,
I still will wait. I wait for you.

# MOSELLE CROW

Dawnlight creeps across vineyards
along the Moselle's chalky slopes
and the heady scent of ripe Riesling grapes
drifts through the window of the hotel
and into my semi-consciousness when
I am yanked to wakefulness
by a familiar raucous cry.

It is Crow — no mistaking
this unmelodic voice, the same here
in this little German village
as anywhere Crow flies. I can't
believe Crow's followed me all this way
just to grate my dreams at German dawn.

Bird of myth and legend. Crow
crosses oceans and mountains,
flies beyond language, through time,
beyond humankind's history of strife.
Like sun, wind and rain Crow is there,
its harsh voice inevitable as death.

BEFORE THE STRIKE

I saw in that millisecond
the giant
     rainbow
         trout
rush the baited hook
jaws agape
      down, down
beyond the eyes' power
to perceive
     deep
in the lake's murky dark.

I swear
    this is true.
Believe it.

    I saw
the sudden rush
      the rose
flash of its silver side
the eyes intent
       and wide.
In the instant
      the great trout
smashed the hook
     and bent
the rod tip
    to the water
I froze.

And the trout spit
the hook
        swirled
            and left me
with just this
            inexplicable
wonder.

# IN MY MOTHER'S EIGHTY-FIFTH YEAR

1.

One day Mother says, "I'll tell you,
it's not much fun getting old."
I have no reason to doubt her.

She has been a constant in my life —
my father gone three decades,
my only brother gone almost one.
Now Mother is old and speaks
of her own death, though always
in oblique terms as if direct
confrontation with this truth
might shock me into silence.

2

Mother moves slowly, with infinite care.
She understands the risks of falls
at her age, the brittleness of bone
nine decades have wrought.
She prepares with care for death.
And since I now am her only son
she prepares me, as she did
for my first day of school,
to accept that day.

3.

Her mind grows fragile.
Sometimes she calls me
by my father's name, or my brother's,
sometimes her oldest brother's,
often by her second husband's.

It embarrasses her when her mind
short-circuits or refuses to recall
a name at all. But this, too,
she has come to accept. And I
must accept it as a foretaste,
though it is hard.


4.

I sometimes ask Mother about my father,
dead now for over thirty years,
about their marriage in Vancouver
in the midst of the Great Depression.
I grasp for details I want to hold:
the smallest of histories,
deeply felt. Sometimes she is
confused, uncertain, then she sorts
through the years and I add pieces —
names, circumstances gleaned from others.
It becomes an imperfect picture,
but something that didn't exist
for me before. I am excavating,
the archaeology of self.

5.

I lead Mother down the steps,
hold the door open for her,
steady her to the car, open
the passenger side door, help
her in, assist with the seatbelt —
this routine reversed when we
return. The child become parent:
Mother become child.

We have travelled together
this well worn circle.
Now, of my children, which
is fated to become my father?
Which my mother?

&#9831; &#9831;

# *from* TODAY I BELONG TO AGNES

CARE ASSESSMENT

The woman from Home Care talks with Mother,
asks her various questions; Mother proffers
quite credible replies and everything is well
until the assessor asks how old Mother is.
"Oh, I'm a hundred years old," Mother says
without the slightest hesitation; she's eleven years
off the mark this time. "Really? One hundred?"
"Oh, yes," Mother smiles her sweetest affirmation
as the other seeks corroboration in her files.

*Now why has Mother decided that today*
*she will be a hundred years old? Was she*
*thinking of her favourite aunt who lived*
*to her hundredth birthday? Has she decided*
*if her aunt could do it why not she? Or is*
*Mother engaging in a bit of harmless sport*
*with this earnest woman, leading her on*
*before her laughter lets the other know*
*she's been duped by an eighty-nine year old?*

I'm leaning toward the latter when the woman
asks Mother to tell her what time it is. "Why?"
Mother wants to know, "Can't you tell time?"

I sense caginess from Mother beyond
the game she may be playing with her opponent.

"Yes, I can. What I want is for you to look
at that clock," and she points at the wall,
"and tell me what time it is right now."

Mother looks at the clock for a few seconds,
then turns to the woman and says, "I don't see
why I should tell you the time, if you can see
the clock perfectly well yourself." Then refuses
to play the match further. But perhaps she knows,
even at this moment, that time has made
an unexpected turn, one she'll not set right,
no matter how she plays the game.

VISITORS

1.

Each Thursday the tall
immaculate man arrives
without fail to visit
his mother, but only
Thursdays.

Newly retired he now
looks for meaning in life
without work,
an organization man
who has lived
a structured life
and will never
bend to chaos.

Still, I'd like to ask
him why it must be
Thursday only;
his mother would
be pleased to see him
any day, frequency
would do no harm,
especially since her days
are swiftly moving
to that moment when
one Thursday she
will no longer give
his afternoon its purpose
and the neat order
of his week will
collapse upon him.

2.

This woman must be a school teacher
because she wants to scold her mother:

*Sit up straight now! Where's your hankie?*
*Tuck in your blouse! Are you listening?*

Is this a daughter's revenge on her mother?
Must it come to this? The daughter can

not help herself, it seems. No matter how
warm her greetings, no matter how much

or little they may have to say to each other,
at some point the visit always comes to this.

Perhaps it is a kind of love, the only kind
these two have ever known, or ever shown.

3.

One woman visits her mother often
and each time the visit ends in tears,
not because one has offended the other,
but because each time they part it is
as if it could be for the very last time;
their hearts well up and overflow.
Each parting leaves no guarantee
of future meetings; instead each
leaving brings them closer to pain,
the emptiness of silence after tears.

4.

Each time this woman comes
she works so hard to hide
how her mother's falling back
to childhood upsets her —
as if somehow this should
not be so, as if someone here
must be responsible for
what she sees happening.
She is not yet ready
to see herself
in her mother's place,
refuses to see
what each of us must see.

## WHAT KEEPS US GOING

With the arrival of each baby boy,
seven great-grandsons in succession,

Mother expressed equal joy for each,
while desire for a baby girl burned.

The long awaited great-granddaughter
arrived three weeks before Mother died.

By this time she often failed
to recognize me, though I visited her

several times each day. She could hear
Death tapping his foot in the next room;

her will to persevere had died sometime
in the weeks of doctors and hospital beds.

But the birth of the baby girl rallied her,
so that nurses kept repeating this news

daily to raise her spirits, if only for a moment
before the event faded into the mystery

of forgotten names and faces of her life,
while Death cleared his throat and tapped . . .

## WOMEN WITHOUT MEN

They have lived much of their lives
with men and now in their final years
they are partnerless survivors.
Some linger in grief and regret
for lovers gone; some cheer
in dark silence their release
from bonds of fear;
some have forgotten those
who shared their beds,
who shared their lives.

Here, in their eighties and nineties
they are a random company:
ancient crones living with memories,
sometimes fleeting and faint,
sometimes sharp with longing,
memories of time when there was
an other, a presence that this place
can not evoke, that this home
of aged strangers have in common
but can never truly share.

THINKING

*I've been thinking a lot lately,*

                    Mother says to me one day.

I assure her this is good, thinking is healthy,
but worrying is something to avoid, knowing that all
her life Mother has been a *worrywart,*

                    her self-description.

*Oh no, I haven't been worrying,*

                    she assures me.
*I can't remember anything to worry about!*

So I ask her what sorts of things she thinks about
and for a time she doesn't answer and I'm afraid
she's either forgotten the question or her subject.

*I've been thinking a lot about Mom and Dad,*

                    she says at last
and I know this from previous visits to be true.

I ask her what she remembers of them now;
over a half-century dead, they lie in the country
churchyard where my own father takes his rest.

*I don't remember much, but I still think of them lots.*
My mother's smile that of a happy child.

LEAVINGS

In her ninety-first year
my mother experiences mysterious
visitations; she doesn't know
exactly when they come,
perhaps while she dozes
in her chair while TV talk shows
blather without her,
but people come and go,
she's very sure,
leaving behind little things
to confuse her:
costume jewelry, magazines,
old watches, letters and cards,
unfamiliar clothing —
things not there before.

One day she discovers
an entire carton of bedding
the mysterious visitor has left —
sheets and pillowcases she
recognizes enough to know
the house and time.

But now she's discovered
this box, part of the restless
rooting and sorting
that is a prelude to her
final move; it has become
a mysterious leaving

of the unseen one who
comes and goes
through her small rooms
with impunity.

And all she can do is
put her house in order.

## EVERYMAN

More than a year, several days a week
I've been a visitor in this care home.
I am so constant the staff anticipates me:
I surprise them only when I do not show.

The residents here have seen me now
so often they can't be sure whether
I am missing husband, son, or brother,
some forgotten family member, or staff.

All they know is that they recognize
my face and I am harmless enough
to be entrusted with family news,
or queried about the latest from home.

I might be a plumber come to fix a tap
for them, electrician or carpet cleaner,
priest or doctor. They do not know
my name; they could call me Everyman.

Agnes brings me her photo album.
I know her only by name. I know
none of her family — a gallery
of perfect strangers. Yet today

Agnes insists I play the role
of family member, attentive as she
haltingly studies first one photo,
then another, summons names

and places from the past, weaves
fragmentary images into a tapestry
of blood and bone that she has lived.
I sit beside her as she speaks.

Her frail voice stumbles as she
seeks in English the words
that would be so easy in Hungarian,
the language of her dreams.

Agnes needs someone to listen
and I am those ears. Though I
am here to visit my mother,
today, I belong to Agnes.

## FLOWERS

I bring flowers to the home —
a torch of pink carnations
or sunny chrysanthemums
to burnish December dullness,
or a blaze of scarlet begonia
to warm them; and the women
cluster round the floral offering,
drawn as teens to a pizza.

I bring flowers for my mother.
At least I tell myself this.
But I am thinking of them all
each time I bear this burst
of spring and it is not
so selfless an act as it
may seem: does not their
prompt pleasure become mine?

Few of them know my name,
so I am the Flower Man who
splashes their days with a rush
of colour and scent that they
may *oooh* and *aaah*, faces
opening like exotic blooms.

GARDEN PARTY

There are four of us sitting on the patio:
Mother, whose short term memory is zero,
another whose mind short-circuits mid-thought,
and the third who is all pragmatism without
a jot of imagination. I am the Mad Hatter
of the group, fuelling conversation
with hints and suggestions. It is either
a Monty Python routine or a Kafka fiction.

"What did you mean by that?"
                              "By what?"
"By your last comment."
                              "What did I say?"
"Don't you remember?"
                              "No, do you?"

There is laughter, not so much because
the humour they are finding is intended,
but it's easier to laugh — and better.
Tears demand comfort and explanations;
laughter needs no justification.

Wisps of intent arise and dissipate
as quickly, unfinished or re-routed
into some nether world of the lost.
The practical one turns to Mother,
asks what the remark by the third means;
but my mother has already forgotten,
so she laughs because they are all
laughing at something none of them
either understands or remembers.
And what better than laughter
to fill the growing silence?

# HOUSES

Some days Mother is convinced this care home
is hers and the other dozen women are here
at her whim or pleasure. They may be amused
or irked, as their own failing minds grapple
with the intricacies of language and intent.

Whenever she is brought up short and told
she does not own the house, nor the table
they all sit around, not even her own room,
she is confused. It doesn't seem right.
*Hasn't her son told her this is her home?*

She once had a house, maybe more than one . . .
Different places, times, have merged and now
she is left with a vague memory of *house*,
something she once owned, but now,
is told is no longer hers, something past.

Some days her house is childhood's farm,
sometimes a small town where she worked
as a cook; at times a tiny bungalow in Burnaby.
Some days *this* house is hers and all houses
have become the one she moves toward.

# LANGUAGE

Mother struggles to express herself.
She begins to say something,
then a word refuses to emerge
from the sewing bag of language
and she gropes for what eludes her
until the thread of intent snaps
and her idea falters, disappears
into the discard heap of beginnings
and seams of unfinished sentences.

But when her cousin greets
her in Norwegian, first language
of childhood chatter, she threads
words with dexterity, while
the second language weakens.
In her ear now are the voices
of her long-dead parents
calling, calling.

My mother, at ninety, become rebel.

She cultivates a fondness
for leaning to one side or the other
in the easy chair or on the sofa
until her head slips nearly parallel
to the floor. She prefers to watch
TV from this unique perspective
and when I ask whether she
would like me to help her
regain uprightness, she chuckles
and says it's all the same,
no matter how you look at it.

The staff claim if you straighten her
she soon resumes her skewed view,
so they've opted to grant her
this eccentric glimpse of life.

I suppose I could insist that she
be more closely supervised and be
compelled to regard life squarely,
head-on, to share the collective sight
of the vertical in a horizontal world,
but secretly I rather relish the notion
of my mother at ninety turning rebel,
anarchist to boot, she who lived
nine decades of beholding life
through straight-ahead spectacles.

My mother, at ninety, twisting
the world sideways
to get a second opinion,
resisting the efforts of all,
even her own son, to return her
to the safe conformity of the masses.

My mother at ninety a mutineer —
That pleases me. It gives me hope.

SNAPSHOTS

Gina brings a double set of prints to show —
family photos, a life she lived in a prairie town
before her memory began its certain shutdown
and her present dissipated in Alzheimer's fog.

She talks me through both sets, not once
realizing she repeats each moment. One print
a tiny white frame house, hers, she remembers,
but is puzzled by the rooftop TV antennae,

thinks this must be a bird feeder they erected.
When she concludes her impromptu show-and-tell,
a double colour print journey through her past,
she unknowingly begins anew and now

the story alters shape and one she identified
as her brother becomes someone new whose name
she can't recall, the white house now her brother's
and in this telling located in another province.

In vain she struggles to retain her own story,
faces and places that each day fade closer to loss.
In time these photographs will no longer be
her life at all, just lifeless bits of gloss.

# TELEVISION AFTERNOON

Of all the programs, the cooking shows
appear to interest and amuse the ladies most.
No Jerry Springer brawling spouses,
but rather, chefs in white tossing pizza dough,
or stuffing pale fillets of sole with concoctions
of mushrooms or tiny shrimp with cheese;
they are impressed with fancy knife-work
on the chopping block, love the colours
of paellas or pilafs, ragouts and jambalayas.

They loll back in their chairs or sofas,
snooze during the commercials and beyond,
but focus on ingredients as if committing
the recipes to recall, though it has deserted them.
Even soundless, the cooking shows still win
over the afternoon soaps and talkfests,
as soups are stirred and bread is baked, a leg
of lamb festooned with cloves of garlic,
red bell peppers stuffed with Basmati rice,
a decadence of chocolate drizzled over pears
poached in Gewurtztraminer, the mute chefs
smiling and gesturing, holding up each
newly garnished plate to the camera —
and to the ladies, who withhold applause
like Russian skating judges, but who
sometimes betray appreciation with smiles
measured with memory and knowing.

# MUSICAL INTERLUDE

I open the door to unexpected
rough-edged fiddle sound, accordion
and acoustic guitar: an old dance
melody in full swing. The reel

(or is it a jig, I can't tell)
swirls up the carpeted steps
from the basement level
to the ladies of the parlour.

They sit in their usual places,
eyes closed, most of them;
they could be asleep, but for
the palpable tapping of feet,

the slight movement of lips
as a tune stirs forgotten lines.
Downstairs three aging musicians,
slowed fingers now groping

once-familiar stops, transform
the home to Saturday dancehall
where each woman awaits a turn
to dance in the arms of the past.

# CARE DOG

The care home dog pads from one
woman to the next; each brief stop
evokes a pat on the head, a stroke,
endearing words, low murmurs.

The dog answers to as many names
as there are women in the home;
yet it knows with animal sureness
not one of these is its own.

Each day the dog performs its role
as object of affection for each
of these now left alone, for whom
this brief touch triggers memory

and the dog reminds them anew
of pets and people that still live
in misty mornings of life past.
The dog betrays nothing of this.

Like dreams the dog comes and goes,
stirring in each one that leans
to ruffle its coat, pet its head,
twinges of the unforgotten.

# WEATHER

Thelma always asks the same question:
"Is it very cold outside?" Or else,
a variation: "Is it nice out there?"

She sits beside the window,
sunlight splashing her
frail shoulders and quavers,

"Is it very cold outside?"
I assure her the weather's fine,
return my attention to Mother.

Thelma is going nowhere today,
so weather is nothing more
than a gambit for attention.

"Is it very cold outside?"
she quakes again  the former
question and answer lost.

This plaintive refrain
is a tiring constant and
at times it tries my patience,

but I answer each tremulous
query as though it were
the first, as though I could

bring sunny days to gardeners,
or timely showers to farmers.
I bring Thelma the weather.

DREAMERS

It is night and the house
is filled with sleep.
In every bed, every room
women lost in dream.

In one room a sleeper
holds a doll received
on her fifth birthday,
Eaton's very finest.

Across the hall another
feels two strong arms hold
her close and cries out
the name of her loss.

One dreams shelling peas
fresh picked in a July garden,
while her neighbour walks
sticky-mouthed at the fair.

A farm wife dreams a dog
chasing cows from the wheat;
another is eavesdropping
on the rural party phoneline.

One dreams a favourite uncle,
killed in the trenches at Vimy;
another shrinks and curls herself
at the fierce hand of her father.

In every room slumber dramas
spin through the darkness
like silent films, reel by reel,
the house a mute theatre.

# HOSPITAL VIGIL

I stand beside her bed,
watch her withered body
rise and fall in fitful sleep

and it is hard. This body
on the bed is not my mother;
my mother has already gone.

This is just a dying woman,
a body to fill the hours
of the doctors and nurses,

a body to fill the charts
with data to analyze
and cost out in dollars,

statistics for the health
of the health care system.
My mother is already gone,

though this covered shape
on the bed rises and falls,
rises and falls, rises and falls.

## LOSING SPEECH

In her ninety-second year
my mother is losing ability
to converse. Increasingly words
elude her, and the originating
thought hides while
she seeks the word.
Conversation now is
a series of opening fragments.
Beginnings become entireties,
remnants of intent. She is
now unlearning language.
Memory, the storehouse
of vocabulary and idiom,
is well into deconstruction;
the tongue falters, turns
sluggish as use lessens
in this inevitable,
this painful
journey into silence.

# HANDS REACHING

*It's better if you don't take their hands,*
the helpful young woman informs me,
*then you won't have the problem*
*of dealing with them*
*when you want to leave.*

Residents hunched in their chairs
extend gnarled hands, veins raised
like cordillera relief maps, call out
to me as I pass. They don't know me,
the name uttered, indistinguishable,
but I am someone in their past
they would like to talk with,
perhaps a touch remembered
and desired again as no other.

*It's better if you don't make eye contact*
*with them,* she adds. *It just encourages them.*
I know she is trying to help me
to avoid moments that have recurred
ad infinitum in her days on staff —
the embarrassed visitors besieged
by nameless elderlies who clutch
and clamber like the capsized. But part
of me is appalled; part of me wants
to stop, take each reaching hand,
stroke that hand and speak
those words we all desire.
The other part obeys the staff,
walks past the wavering hands,
past the clamour of voices that call,
and call long after I leave.

# THE NIGHT MY MOTHER DIED

What I remember now
was how she slipped away
so quietly, without fanfare,
the way she lived her life —
no drama, no blinding lights
to set the eyelids aflutter,
no least flicker of recognition
that she saw the brilliant stairs
that marked her passage,
no last deep indrawn Oh!
Nothing. She stopped breathing.

I watched all her life fall
back into the dark cave that was
her open mouth, taking with it
my first squall and all six decades
of my life, all collapsed and falling
into the mystery of her leaving
and the void in all the places
she had been, the greatest
of these voids in me.

֍ ֎